CRAFTING WITH

CLAY POTS

Easy Designs for Flowers, Home Décor, Storage, and More

Peg Couch

DESIGN ORIGINALS

an Imprint of Fox Chapel Publishing

www.d-originals.com

CONTENTS

INTRODUCTION:
CREATIVE CLAY POTS

If you are looking for an easy, inexpensive, and versatile craft—look no further! Terra-cotta (or clay) pots are a blank canvas that can be decorated in many different ways. You can find several books on making adorable pot projects for kids, but in this book, we are going to dress up our pots to create stylish projects that make wonderful gifts and home accents.

No matter what your level of crafting experience, you can create something beautiful with clay pots. Their smooth surface is wonderful for painting and embellishing. You can keep your pots simple or you can add layers of texture to create something more intricate.

Inside this book, you'll find pot designs for every occasion—from a snazzy caddy for entertaining to a French-inspired lavender pot, from chalkboard paint herb pots to a tiered treat stand, you will find on-trend looks to suit your style.

Come on, let's get started!

ABOUT CLAY POTS

Clay pots come in a wide range of sizes, from mini 2" (5cm) pots through to large 10" (25.5cm) pots and beyond. You can find clay pots at most craft stores, as well as flower nurseries and many mass retailers. Most stores carry the standard flowerpot shape, but be sure to keep an eye out for any unique sizes or shapes that might suit the style of your project.

Clay pot sizes are not always exact, and the measurements listed on the pots can vary by store. Ultimately, the projects in the book can be made in any size you'd like. The measurements listed here are general guidelines to give you an idea of the sizes used in this book. All measurements refer to the approximate diameter of the pot opening. The projects will simply refer to the pots as extra small, small, medium, etc.

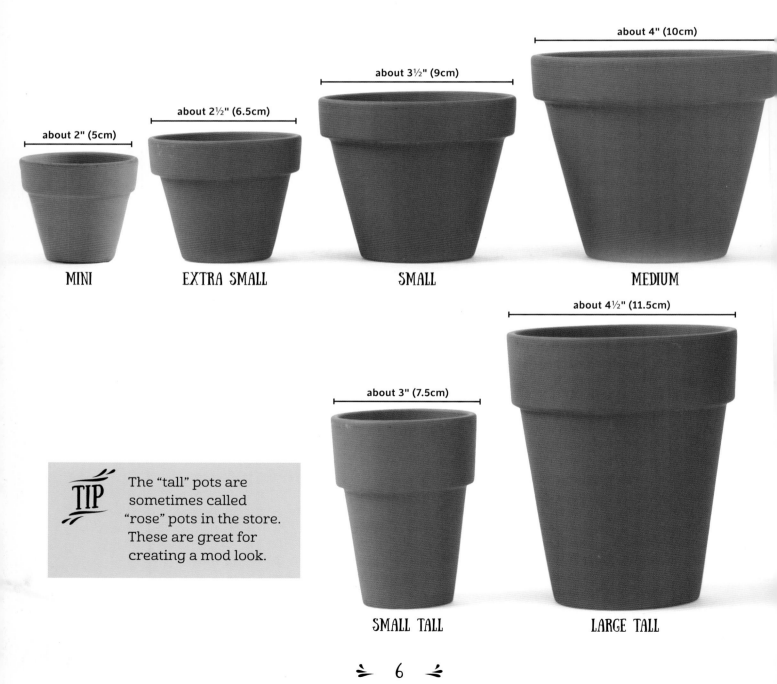

about 2" (5cm)

MINI

about 2½" (6.5cm)

EXTRA SMALL

about 3½" (9cm)

SMALL

about 4" (10cm)

MEDIUM

about 3" (7.5cm)

SMALL TALL

about 4½" (11.5cm)

LARGE TALL

TIP The "tall" pots are sometimes called "rose" pots in the store. These are great for creating a mod look.

about 6" (15cm)

about 8" (20.5cm)

LARGE

EXTRA LARGE

Clay Pot Saucers

Saucers for clay pots are typically sold separately and come in sizes that coordinate with the pots. If you plan to plant flowers in your pot, it is very important to purchase the corresponding saucer to avoid water damage to any surfaces when hydrating your plant. For crafting, the saucers are essential as they provide another surface to decorate and embellish!

Before purchasing, make sure you set your pot in your saucer to make sure they pair nicely. You don't want to arrive home to find you have a saucer that looks overly large or small with your chosen pot!

Clay saucers usually come in diameters that match the opening of their corresponding pot. For example, a large pot with a 6" [15cm]-diameter opening will have a matching 6" [15cm] saucer.

ABOUT PAINT

Clay pots are a perfect canvas for paint. The smooth surface makes the painting process thoroughly enjoyable, and the porous clay helps the paint dry quickly. And the end result is always fabulous! There are so many wonderful paint products on the market. Here are a few favorites for clay pots.

Acrylic paint. All-purpose acrylic paints are a must-have for painting clay pots. These paints provide good coverage, blend well, and clean up easily. They are widely available and come in dozens of colors and fun finishes, such as metallic and glitter. Best of all, they are inexpensive.

Exterior craft paint. Products like Patio Paint are designed specifically for concrete, wood, and terra-cotta. The paint is weather resistant, making it a great choice for any projects you will be displaying outdoors. The paint goes on beautifully and will hold up well over time.

Spray paint. Spray paint goes on quickly and is perfect for a quick pot project. Work in a well-ventilated area and cover your work surface with newspaper to protect it from overspray. Apply two to three thin coats (to avoid dripping) and allow time for the pot to dry thoroughly after each application.

Chalkboard paint. This is a favorite for any craft project! Create a timeless look with classic matte black, or look for other fun colors for a unique twist. The paint is a breeze to apply and clings to the pot's surface very well. Let the paint dry completely and then have fun personalizing the finished pot with chalk.

Chalk-finish paint. Not to be confused with chalkboard paint, chalk-finish paint comes in a variety of colors and has a matte finish that gives your project the aged, rustic look of a French antique. This type of paint is now widely available at an affordable price in craft stores.

High-gloss paint. This product has super shine! It goes beyond a regular gloss finish—high-gloss paint will make your average clay pot look like an expensive ceramic piece. If you are going for a decorator's finish or modern look, this is the perfect product. Maxx Gloss paint was used for the projects in this book.

Paint pens. Once your base paint is applied, get creative and embellish your project with paint pens. They come in a variety of colors and point sizes. Use them to personalize your pots with words, monograms, and labels. Or, use them to add a pop of interest with polka dots and other patterns.

Different paints will give your pots different looks. High-gloss paint (left) is upscale and sophisticated. Acrylic paint (right) comes in multitudes of colors and pairs well with any style.

Paint pens allow you to add your own unique, personalized designs to any pot. For beginners, the pens are much easier to use than paintbrushes, meaning you can apply intricate designs without hassle.

SPRAY PAINT

ACRYLIC PAINT

CHALKBOARD PAINT

EXTERIOR CRAFT
PAINT

HIGH-GLOSS PAINT

CHALK-FINISH PAINT

PAINT PENS

PREP AND PAINT TIPS

Here are some helpful tips and tricks to ensure your success when painting clay pots. Pay particular attention to the paint prep section—a very important step to make sure your paint finish and color come out exactly as you want!

Prepping Your Pot

It is very tempting to just jump in and start painting your pots as soon as you get them, but it really pays to do a little prep work! Prepping your pot won't take long at all, and it will ensure your finish looks the way you intended and will last over time. Also consider that pots sometimes come with a dusty residue that you'll want to remove for a fresh painting surface. Here are some quick and easy steps to get your pot ready for crafting.

1. **Remove labels.** Peel any stickers or price tags off the pot surface.
2. **Sand lightly.** Using fine-grit sandpaper, smooth the inside and outside of the pot. Be sure to sand off any residue left behind from any stickers.
3. **Wipe down.** Wipe the entire surface of your pot with a damp, soft cloth and let it dry.
4. **Seal.** If you plan to paint the outside of your pot, seal the *inside* with a water-based terra-cotta sealer (found anywhere clay pots are sold). This will block moisture from seeping through the walls of the pot from the inside out and damaging the paint finish on the exterior.
5. **Prime.** For the best results, always prime your pots with a water-based primer before painting. When you prime, your chosen paint color will appear much truer to what you see on the package, the paint will go on smoother, and you will use less of it.

TERRA-COTTA SEALER

PRIMER

CLEAR ACRYLIC FINISH

Taking the time to seal, prime, and finish your pots will ensure your finished project looks great and lasts.

Painting Tips

- **Test your paint.** Depending on the color and type of paint you are using, it may look different on the pot than it does in the bottle. Test a small stroke on the bottom of your pot to see the color as it will appear on the pot.
- **Prime your pots.** If you have tested your paint and are not happy with the finished color, prime your pot with a water-based primer and test again. Applying your paint to a primed pot should result in a color that's much truer to that in the paint bottle.
- **Seal your pots.** Use a water-based sealer to coat the inside of your pot so that water will not seep through the walls from the inside out and ruin your paint job.
- **Use the proper paint.** If you plan to display your pot outdoors, use an appropriate weather-resistant paint, such as Patio Paint. This paint is designed to protect your finish and goes on beautifully.
- **Purchase enough paint.** Clay pots are porous and soak up a lot of paint, so if you are painting a large project or several pots in the same color, be sure to purchase extra paint. Two small bottles of acrylic paint (2 fl oz [59 ml]) are typically enough to apply two coats of paint to an extra large pot, but it never hurts to have extra on hand, just in case!
- **Apply enough coats.** Some paints provide enough coverage after one coat, but your finished project will look much more polished if you apply two coats (and possibly three for light colors). Plus, you can use that second coat to touch up any areas you're not quite happy with after your first pass.

- **Paint everywhere.** For most projects it's not absolutely necessary to paint the bottom or inside of your pot, but why not? Painting every surface of your pot will give your finished project some extra polish. And you will avoid last-minute touch-ups after you finish and realize an area you didn't think would be visible actually is!
- **Test your brush.** Foam brushes are great for painting pots, as they will not leave distinct brush marks behind, but be sure to test a variety of options and use the brush that feels the most comfortable and works for you. For fine details, such as polka dots or lettering, you will want a thin artist's liner brush.
- **Prop your pot.** For hands-free painting, place your pot (upside down) over a can or other appropriately sized item so that you can paint all sides easily. This way, you can paint your pot without having to hold it and can let it dry without touching any surfaces.
- **Tape it off.** Use painter's tape or Frog Tape to cover any areas that you do not wish to be painted. Use this resist technique to create fun patterns like diamonds or chevrons.
- **Protect your finish.** After painting your pot (and before adding any embellishments like ribbon or beads), spray on a light coat of clear acrylic finish in matte or gloss, depending on the desired look. Be sure to do this in a well-ventilated area.

 Terra-cotta is a porous surface that will absorb moisture, including paint. An unsealed pot will allow moisture from watering to seep through to the outside, damaging any finish you apply to the pot's exterior. An unprimed pot will soak up the paint you apply, which can distort the color and means you will have to apply more coats. This is especially true for metallic and light-colored paints. So take the time to prime!

TOOLS AND MATERIALS

Crafting with clay pots is so much fun because there are endless ways to decorate, embellish, and assemble them. They really are the most hardworking craft surface available! From scrapbook paper, to ribbon, to faux flowers and beyond—you can find inspiration everywhere. And when it comes to tools, you don't need loads of equipment—just a few staple items. Below is an overview of some of the materials, embellishments, and tools we will use in this book.

Scrapbook paper. Scrapbook paper has many applications when working with clay pots. Découpage it over the entire pot, or trim smaller motifs from your paper to create a one-of-a-kind design. Use coordinating bits of scrapbook paper to embellish gift tags to add to your pot if gifting it to a friend.

Stencils. Stencils come in many sizes, shapes, and patterns—there is something to fit every style! Be sure to measure the size of the stencil to ensure it will fit properly on your pot. Look for stencils that are specifically made for garden pots, as they are specially designed to stick to the curved surface of the pot.

Beads and bling. Sometimes you need a few special details to take your pot design to the next level. Look in the jewelry aisle as well as the sticker aisle, where you will find loads of stick-on rhinestones. Look for the ones that come in preset strips, making them very easy to apply. These and other jewelry aisle finds are perfect for adding a little sparkle.

Wooden accessories. From small tags to precut shapes like birds, letters, and more, you can find a lot of really cute accessories to personalize your pots in the wood aisle of your craft store. All you need is a little paint and some imagination!

Knobs. One of the most popular things to do with clay pots is to use the saucers as lids by turning them upside down and placing them on top of the pots. This is where knobs come in! You can hot glue a knob to the center of your saucer/lid to make a functional and stylish handle to open your pot.

Floral accents. Faux flowers, preserved moss, and other floral accents are natural materials for crafting with clay pots. Look for pretty blossoms to make topiaries for your next event (see page 36).

Ribbon and trim. Here is a perfect way to add style and personality to your pot projects. Burlap will give you a rustic chic look, silk ribbon is perfect for a simple sweet and pretty look, and hemp, rope, or sasil are great for a beachy vibe. Get really creative and try découpaging lace onto your pot for an updated look that is feminine but not too precious.

Hot glue gun and glue sticks. There are lots and lots of adhesives on the market, each with their own special qualities and materials they pair well with. However, the hardworking glue gun is a staple item that pairs well with just about anything.

Cutting tools. In addition to standard craft scissors, a smaller pair of scissors can come in handy for making detailed cuts on scrapbook paper and other items. Additionally, a pair of inexpensive wire cutters will be very helpful if/when you are working with faux flowers.

Paintbrushes. When it comes to clay pots, foam brushes are the best. The paint goes on smoothly with them and does not drip or streak. If you are working on a large project, you may wish to use a large paintbrush. If so, try applying the base layer of paint with the paintbrush and apply the final coat with a foam brush so your topcoat is nice and smooth. Small liner brushes are great for hand lettering and adding small elements like polka dots, etc.

There are so many crafting supplies available. Use this book as inspiration. Try a few of the projects inside, and soon you will have your own creative ideas. Go bold with colors and materials. Make it pretty and make it you— it's all about having fun!

STEP-BY-STEP
PROJECTS

She Said Yes! Gift Pot

MATERIALS

Large tall clay pot

Medium clay saucer

Wooden gift tag blank

Tan scrapbook paper

White faux flower

⅜" (10mm) burlap ribbon

Light green acrylic paint

White paint pen

Hot glue gun and glue sticks

Brushes

Scissors

Wire cutters

Here is a special way to wrap your next bridal shower or wedding gift. Simply paint your pot, add your small gift, and decorate with ribbon, flowers, and a cute tag. This also makes a great favor! Be sure you pay extra attention when purchasing the saucer for this project, as it will act as the lid, so you want it to be a perfect fit!

1 **Paint the surfaces.** Paint your clay pot, saucer, and wooden tag with two coats of light green acrylic paint. Allow the paint to dry thoroughly between coats and after the final coat.

2 **Prepare the gift tag.** Using your wooden tag as a guide, cut a paper insert slightly smaller than the tag from the scrapbook paper. Write your message on the paper with a white paint pen and glue it onto your wooden tag.

3 **Attach the flower topper.** Remove the stem from your faux flower with wire cutters. Attach the flower to the bottom of your saucer with hot glue.

4 **Embellish, stuff, and assemble.** Place your gift in the painted pot and add the saucer lid with flower embellishment on top. Use burlap ribbon to hold the lid on the pot and attach your gift tag.

TIP This is a great way to make giving gift cards more personal. Just pop the card inside the pot and add a packet of flower seeds for an extra-special touch!

Lavender Herb Pot

MATERIALS

Large clay pot

Large clay saucer

Wooden tag blank

¼" (0.5cm) wooden dowel

White chalk-finish paint

Metallic silver paint pen

Hot glue gun and glue sticks

Brushes

Sandpaper or handsaw

Potting soil

Lavender plant

Vive la France! An ordinary clay pot takes on the look of an aged European antique with a simple layer of white chalk-finish paint. Add a touch of whimsy with a hand-painted embellishment in metallic silver.

1 **Paint the surfaces.** Paint your clay pot, saucer, wooden tag, and dowel with two layers of white chalk-finish paint. Allow the paint to dry thoroughly between coats and after the final coat.

2 **Embellish the pot.** Using a metallic silver paint pen, embellish your pot as desired. You can use the templates on page 48 to add laurel branches, the Eiffel Tower, and an inscription, or create your own design!

3 **Prepare the tag.** Using your metallic silver paint pen, add the word "Provence" (region in southeastern France), or another word of your choice, to the tag. Allow the paint to dry. Glue the tag onto one end of the wooden dowel with hot glue. Sand or cut the other end of the dowel to form a point.

4 **Assemble.** Fill your pot halfway with potting soil, add your lavender plant, and fill the remaining area with potting soil. Water lightly. Insert your wooden tag and enjoy.

 TIP Set your lavender plant in a sunny location and water it lightly. Enjoy the beautiful fragrance!

Baby Shower Gumball Pots

MATERIALS

2 medium clay pots

2 medium clay saucers

Two 1" (2.5cm) wooden knobs

Two 4" (10cm) round glass
candleholders or bowls

Round candy (to look like gumballs)

¾" (20mm) light pink ribbon

¾" (20mm) light blue ribbon

2 stick-on rhinestones

Metallic light pink acrylic paint

Metallic light blue acrylic paint

Hot glue gun and glue sticks

Brushes

Scissors

What a fun idea for your next baby shower! These little gumball cuties are not only great centerpieces, they make great favors, too. A small glass candleholder provides a creative vessel to fill with candy.

1 **Paint the surfaces.** Paint your clay pots, saucers, and knobs—one set in metallic light pink and the other in metallic light blue. You will need to apply at least two coats (and possibly a third) to avoid streaking. Allow the paint to dry thoroughly between coats and after the final coat.

2 **Attach the glass bowls.** Turn the pots upside down and apply a ring of hot glue around the center hole of each pot. Place each glass bowl on top of the hot glue and allow the glue to set. It is good to hold the bowls in place as the glue sets to keep them from slipping out of place.

3 **Attach the knobs.** Turn your saucers upside down and apply a small dot of hot glue in the center of each saucer. Place the flat end of each knob on the glue and allow it to set. Place a stick-on rhinestone on the top of each knob.

4 **Fill, assemble, and embellish.** Fill each glass bowl with your chosen candy, and place a saucer lid on top of each bowl. Embellish each gumball pot with a pink and blue ribbon bow to cover the area where the bowl meets the pot.

 TIP Apply some extra primer to your pots when using metallic paint, and especially when using light colors like the ones for this project. The primer will prevent the paint from soaking into the pot, meaning the paint will go on better, be less streaky, and require fewer coats.

Glam Vanity Caddy

MATERIALS

Large tall clay pot

Medium clay saucer

Sheets of stick-on rhinestone strips (as many as desired)

Metallic silver spray paint

What little girl would not swoon over this bedazzled caddy? Perfect for brushes, hair accessories, and more, this caddy is stylish and handy. Add a little rhinestone bling to compacts and other accessories to create a coordinating set.

1 Paint the surfaces. Paint your pot and saucer with metallic silver spray paint. Be sure to work in a well-ventilated area and apply the paint in thin coats to avoid dripping. Allow the paint to dry thoroughly between coats and after the final coat.

2 Apply the rhinestones to the pot. Attach your stick-on rhinestones in rows to cover the entire rim of your pot.

3 Apply the rhinestones to the saucer. Attach your stick-on rhinestones in rows to cover the entire edge of your saucer.

4 Embellish the accessories. Using the leftover rhinestones, embellish your chosen accessories, such as a brush, compact, and other vanity items, to create a coordinating set.

TIP Stick-on rhinestones come in a variety of formats. Look for wide strips of rhinestones to avoid having to apply individual stones. You can also get creative and try different shapes and colored stones.

Polka Dot Cupcake Pots

MATERIALS

Mini clay pots (as many as desired)

Pink acrylic paint

White acrylic paint

Brushes

Cotton swabs

Mini cupcakes

Pink sprinkles or other edible decorations

Here is an easy and inexpensive way to punch up the cute factor at your next birthday party, baby shower, or girls' night. After you've enjoyed the cupcakes, wash out the pots and use them to organize small craft or office supplies.

1 **Paint the surfaces.** Paint inside and outside of your pots with two coats of pink acrylic paint. Allow the paint to dry thoroughly between coats and after the final coat.

2 **Apply the polka dots.** Dip a clean cotton swab into your white paint and blot it to remove the excess. Gently press the tip of the swab onto the surface of the pots to form perfect polka dots.

3 **Continue adding polka dots.** Continue to dip, blot, and dab your swab all around each pot until you have covered it with polka dots.

4 **Add the cupcakes.** Gently "drop" a cupcake into each pot and cover with pink sprinkles or other edible decorations.

 TIP Mini cupcakes work beautifully for the mini pots shown, but you can also use larger pots for larger cupcakes! To remove the cupcake, simply tilt the pot and gently shake it until you can grasp the cupcake wrapper to pull the cupcake out.

Chalkboard Herb Pots

MATERIALS

3 large clay pots

3 large clay saucers

Black chalkboard paint

White paint pen (or chalk)

Brushes

Potting soil

Sage plant

Thyme plant

Mint plant

This project is so easy and inexpensive, yet packs a lot of style! Look for chalkboard paint at your local craft store. It is one of the easiest paints to apply to clay pots—it clings to the clay and dries with a lovely, smooth finish. These pots are a beautiful way to display your kitchen herb garden.

1 **Paint the surfaces.** Paint all of your pots and saucers with two coats of black chalkboard paint. Allow the paint to dry thoroughly between coats and after the final coat.

2 **Label the pots.** Using your white paint pen (or chalk), write the name of an herb onto the front of each pot. You can use the templates provided on page 48, or freehand the labels.

3 **Assemble.** Fill each pot halfway with potting soil. Add the corresponding plant to each pot and fill the remaining area with potting soil. Water lightly. Move the pots to a sunny place and enjoy fresh herbs anytime!

TIP This is a versatile project that can be adapted for many uses. If you don't have a green thumb, use the pots as organizational caddies. Kids' toys, craft or office supplies, and more can be corralled neatly and stylishly in chalkboard clay pots.

TIP Handwriting not perfect? No problem! Label your pots with chalk instead of a permanent paint pen. That way, you can erase and recreate your label until you are satisfied with the results, or change the label when the pot takes on a new use!

Stacked Garden Pots

MATERIALS

Medium clay pot (make sure this fits, upside down, into the bottom of the extra large pot)

Large clay pot

Extra large clay pot

Super large saucer (about 10" [25.5cm])

Red acrylic paint

White paint pen

Hot glue gun and glue sticks

Brushes

Potting soil

2 varieties of annual plants (spill and fill, see tip at right)

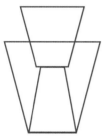

Assembly Diagram

Punch up your curb appeal with clay pots! This attention-grabbing tiered pot is a cheerful way to welcome neighbors and guests. Change the paint color to coordinate with your home and add your own name and house number.

1 Paint the surfaces. Paint your extra large pot, large pot, and saucer with two coats of red (or your desired color) acrylic paint. Leave the medium pot unfinished. Allow the paint to dry thoroughly between coats and after the final coat.

2 Personalize. Using the white paint pen, add your house number to the front of the extra large pot and your family name to the front of the large pot.

3 Assemble the pots. Place the extra large pot on the saucer. Turn the medium pot upside down and place it inside the extra large pot. Apply a ring of hot glue around the center hole on the bottom of the medium pot. Place the large pot on top of the hot glue and allow it to set. (See diagram at left.)

4 Add the plants. Fill the bottom pot with potting soil (fill to about 2" [5cm] below the bottom of the rim). Insert spilling annual plants around the circumference and fill the remaining area with more potting soil. Fill the top pot halfway with potting soil. Add your feature annual plants and fill the remaining area with potting soil. Water lightly and enjoy!

For best results, use a paint specifically designed for outdoor use.

TIP The key to a beautiful container plant is to pot with a spiller and a filler! Spillers are cascading plants that will hang below the lip of the pot, such as ivy or potato vine. Fillers are flowering plants that add mass and complement the filler, such as impatiens or marigolds. For an over-the-top effect, add a third pot to this design with a "thriller" plant—a tall, bold centerpiece to draw the eye.

Entertaining Caddy

MATERIALS

3 large clay pots

18" x 5" (45.5 x 12.5cm) wooden tray

3 chalkboard labels (can substitute any black label)

Matte black acrylic paint

Matte tan acrylic paint

White paint pen (or chalk)

Brushes

Step up the style at your next party with this sophisticated utensil caddy, inspired by looks seen in upscale home décor catalogs. The chalk labels and coordinating black tray add a bold punch to this functional and fabulous project.

1 Paint the surfaces. Paint the inside only of the clay pots with two coats of matte black paint. Allow the paint to dry thoroughly between coats and after the final coat. Paint the exterior of the pots with two coats of matte tan paint, allowing each coat to dry thoroughly.

2 Paint the tray. Paint all surfaces of the wooden tray with two coats of matte black paint. Allow the paint to dry thoroughly between coats and after the final coat.

3 Prepare the labels. Use the white paint pen (or chalk) to write the name of a utensil on each of the three labels: Spoons, Knives, Forks.

4 Assemble. Place each label on the front of a pot. Fill the pots with utensils and line them up on the tray. Enjoy!

Menu

Salad
Mixed Greens Garden Salad with Tomato Vinaigrette

Dinner
Chicken Tuscany
Grilled & Seasoned Focaccia
Italian Vegetable Blend

Dessert
Raspberry & Peach Pies
Assortment of Cookies

forks   Spoons   knives

TIP Use a little burlap to add a designer's touch and fill your pots. Alternatively, you can wrap disposable dinnerware in pretty coordinating napkins and tie each set with natural cord for a rustic-chic look.

Rope-Wrapped Hurricane Pot

Large tall clay pot

Medium clay saucer

¼" (5mm) white rope

Décor sand

White pillar candle

Glass hurricane lantern

Navy blue acrylic paint

White paint pen

Hot glue gun and glue sticks

Brushes

Scissors

Duct tape

Light up any room with the cozy ambience of this nautical hurricane lamp. Made from a large tall clay pot and outfitted with a glass shade, this project is inexpensive and easy. It makes a great centerpiece for a summer barbecue and outdoor entertaining.

1 Paint the surfaces. Paint the clay pot and saucer with two coats of navy blue paint. Allow the paint to dry thoroughly between coats and after the final coat.

2 Paint the anchor. Using the white paint pen, add an anchor to the front of the pot. You can use the template provided on page 48, or freehand the design. Allow the paint to dry completely.

3 Apply the rope. Cover the end of the rope with a dab of hot glue to prevent fraying. Apply a ring of hot glue around the pot's rim, as close to the top as possible. Place the rope on top of the glue to create the first row. Make sure the end of the rope is at the back of the pot. Continue working in rows, adding glue and then rope until the entire top rim of the pot is covered. When finished, trim away the excess rope at the back of the pot and add a dab of hot glue to secure the end. Also add one row of rope to the edge of the saucer.

4 Fill and assemble. Cut a small piece of duct tape and place it inside your pot, covering the hole in the bottom. Fill the pot three-quarters full with décor sand (or more depending on your hurricane lantern). Add the white pillar candle. Cover the candle with a hurricane lantern.

TIP For an alternative beach look, paint your pot white and cover the rim with natural roping or sisal. Talk about coastal chic!

Coastal Mosaic Pot

MATERIALS

Medium clay pot

Medium clay saucer

Sea foam green acrylic paint

⅜" (1cm) precut mosaic tiles in blue and green (approximately 250, depending on pattern)

1 container mosaic grout

Grout spreader

Brushes

Sponge

Potting soil

Coordinating plant

This classic mosaic pot, in pretty hues of blue and green, conjures up the feeling of a relaxing day at the beach. If you have never tried mosaics, you'll be surprised at just how easy and fun they are to make.

1 **Paint the surfaces.** Paint the pot and saucer with two coats of sea foam green paint. Allow the paint to dry thoroughly between coats and after the final coat.

2 **Apply the tiles.** Prepare the mosaic grout following the manufacturer's instructions. Working in small sections, use a small spreader to apply a thin layer of grout to the pot. Then, place your tiles in the desired pattern. Cover the pot body (from the bottom of the rim to the bottom of the pot) with tiles.

3 **Apply the grout.** After the tiles have set, apply a thick coat of grout over the entire surface of the tiled area. Use the spreader to ensure the grout goes into all crevices. Use a damp sponge to wipe the entire surface, removing grout from the tile fronts, but ensuring it remains in the crevices. Allow everything to dry thoroughly.

4 **Assemble.** Fill the pot halfway with potting soil. Add your plant and fill the remaining area with potting soil. Water lightly.

TIP Create a collection of coordinating pots by using tiles of the same color, but arranging them in different patterns.

Blooming Topiary Pots

MATERIALS

2 large clay pots

About 4 pink silk flowers with long stems and multiple blooms (about 30–40 individual blooms per flower)

Four 5" (12.5cm)-diameter foam balls

One 108.5in³ (1777.9cm³) package preserved moss

White chalk-finish paint

Hot glue gun and glue sticks

Brushes

Wire cutters

Topiaries add a touch of elegance to any décor, but they can be very expensive. Now, you can create your own easy and inexpensive clay pot topiaries. These make a perfect centerpiece for dinner parties and other special occasions.

1 Paint the surfaces. Paint both clay pots with two layers of white chalk-finish paint. Allow the paint to dry thoroughly between coats and after the final coat.

2 Prepare the flowers. Using wire cutters, remove individual blooms from the flower stems. Set the stems aside. Then, attach each bloom to a foam ball using hot glue. Allow the glue to set completely. Insert the stem from one of your flowers into the ball. Make sure the stem is thick enough to support the weight of the ball.

3 Fill the pots. Place a foam ball in each clay pot. Add dabs of hot glue to ensure stability. Insert the other end of the stem with the floral ball attached into the ball inside the pot so that it stands upright. Repeat for the second pot.

4 Apply the moss. Using hot glue, gently apply bits of moss to cover the foam ball inside each pot. Work in small sections, ensuring that each bit of moss is secure and that all of the foam is covered.

TIP For a totally different look, replace the pink blooms with faux boxwood branches. This will give you the upscale look of an English garden in your own home.

Floral Découpage Pot

MATERIALS

Large clay pot

Large clay saucer

Floral scrapbook paper

Light blue acrylic paint

Découpage medium

Brushes

Scissors

Potting soil

Coordinating plant

This is a perfect example of how easy it is to personalize your space with clay pot crafting. For this project, all you need is a pot, some paint, scrapbook paper of your choice, and découpage medium. You can create an entire collection of pretty pots for your home and also give them away as gifts.

1 Paint the surfaces. Paint your clay pot and saucer with two coats of light blue acrylic paint. Allow the paint to dry thoroughly between coats and after the final coat.

2 Prepare the paper. Study your scrapbook paper and find a motif to cut out for découpaging. Dry fit the cut paper on your pot to ensure that you are satisfied with the way it looks.

3 Découpage. Apply a thin layer of découpage medium over the entire surface of your pot. While the medium is still wet, gently press the scrapbook paper in place and allow everything to dry. Brush a layer of découpage medium over the applied paper. Be sure to work slowly so your paper does not move or tear. If bubbles appear, use your finger to smooth them out, working from the center outward. Add a final layer of decoupage medium over the entire surface of the pot.

4 Assemble. Place your pot onto its saucer. Fill the pot halfway with potting soil. Add the plant of your choice and fill the remaining area with potting soil. Water lightly.

 TIP For another fun découpage technique, try using bits of fabric instead of scrapbook paper. You can cover the entire pot or use small elements. The options are endless!

Boho Lace Pots

MATERIALS

Large tall clay pot

Small tall clay pot

1" (25mm)-wide lace trim

Découpage medium

Brushes

Scissors

Potting soil

Gravel

Aquarium stones

Succulent plants

Create a modern, bohemian look with a collection of potted planters embellished with pretty lace trim. It's a feminine but earthy look that works really well with succulent plants.

1 Prepare the trim. Cut lace trim into strips. You will need 6 strips, 6" (15cm) long, for the small pot and 8 strips, 8" (20.5cm) long, for the large pot.

2 Apply the découpage medium. Apply a base coat of découpage medium over the entire surface of both pots. Allow it to dry.

3 Apply the lace. Cover the bottom of a pot with découpage medium and attach one end of each strip of lace to the bottom, spacing the pieces evenly. Allow everything to dry. Working with one lace strip at a time, apply the découpage medium from the bottom to the top of the pot, and over the rim to the inside. Gently pull each strip of lace to the top of the pot, pressing it against the découpage medium, and secure the end on the inside of the rim. Repeat until all of your strips are attached, and allow everything to dry. Apply a final coat of découpage medium over the lace and the pot. Repeat for the second pot.

4 Assemble. Fill the pots three-quarters full with a mix of potting soil and gravel. Add the succulents and finish with a layer of aquarium stones.

TIP   When planting your succulent, be sure the plant sits above the rim of the pot once planted. Add additional soil mix to your pot as necessary to ensure your plant gets the proper placement.

Stenciled Candleholder

MATERIALS

Medium clay pot

Medium clay saucer

Stencils (made for garden pots)

White pillar candle

Aquarium stones or crushed shells

Orange acrylic paint

White acrylic paint

Hot glue gun and glue sticks

Brushes

Foam dauber

Add warmth and atmosphere to any room in the house with this adorable candleholder. A stencil specifically designed for garden pots was used to create the painted detail on this piece. Garden pot stencils are made to cling to the pot's curved surface, making the crafting so easy!

1 Paint the surfaces. Paint the pot and saucer with two coats of orange acrylic paint. Allow the paint to dry thoroughly between coats and after the final coat.

2 Plan the pattern. Study your stencils and plan where you want the designs to appear on your pot. Place the first stencil on the pot.

3 Paint the stencil. Using a foam dauber, apply thin coats of white acrylic paint over the stencil, covering all the open spaces. Apply a minimum of two coats and possibly three to achieve an opaque finish, allowing each coat to dry thoroughly. Repeat to add more stencils as desired.

4 Glue and assemble. Apply a ring of hot glue around the top edge of the pot. Place the saucer, right side up, on top of the ring of glue and let it set. Fill the saucer with aquarium stones or crushed shells and add the pillar candle.

TIP When it comes to these adorable candleholders, the more the merrier! Make multiples to fill a room with ambience. Try using multiple pot sizes with the same paint color for variety and interest.

High-Gloss Bathroom Caddy

MATERIALS

Large tall clay pot

Small tall clay pot

3 medium clay saucers

Glass knob

High-gloss blue paint

Cotton balls

Cotton swabs

Bar soap

Hot glue gun and glue sticks

Brushes

No more messes in the bathroom! This little project is adorable as well as handy. The pretty glass knob and high-gloss shine add a bit of style to this set.

1 Paint the surfaces. Paint each pot and saucer with two coats of high-gloss blue paint. Work in thin layers to ensure the paint does not drip. Allow the paint to dry between coats. If necessary, add a third coat and allow the paint to dry completely.

2 Attach the knob. Turn one of the saucers upside down and apply a dot of hot glue in the center. Place the bottom of the glass knob on the glue and allow it to set. Hold the knob in place to ensure it does not slide. If necessary, use a cotton swap to remove any excess glue around the base of the knob.

3 Assemble the set. Use hot glue to secure the large pot to the center of one of the remaining saucers.

4 Fill the containers. Fill the large pot with cotton balls and the small pot with cotton swabs. Use the remaining saucer as a soap dish or a tray to store jewelry or other items.

 TIP Further personalize this caddy collection with stickers—they are not just for kids anymore! Look for monograms, labels, and pretty designs. You can also find repositionable stickers that you can color to create a totally unique look!

Treat Tower Tiered Stand

MATERIALS

Large tall clay pot

Small tall clay pot

Extra small clay pot

Super large clay saucer (about 10" [25.5cm])

Large clay saucer

Medium clay saucer

Mini clay saucer

Purple acrylic paint

Green acrylic paint

White paint pen

Hot glue gun and glue sticks

Brushes

Cupcakes, cookies, or other treats

Going up? Take your party to the next level with this multitiered treat stand. This is a great project for the kids to help with, and they're likely to enjoy making it as much as taking from it!

1 Paint the pots. Paint the pots with two coats of purple paint. Allow the paint to dry thoroughly between coats and after the final coat.

2 Paint the saucers. Paint the saucers with two coats of green paint. Allow the paint to dry thoroughly between coats and after the final coat.

3 Add embellishments. Using the white paint pen, add a line of polka dots around the rim of each saucer.

4 Assemble. Assemble the stand by stacking the pots and saucers, centering them on top of one another, and securing each piece with hot glue. Stack and secure the pieces in the following order: super large saucer, large tall pot (upside down), large saucer, small tall pot (upside down), medium saucer, extra small pot (upside down), mini saucer. Allow the glue to set thoroughly. Fill the stand with cupcakes and other treats and enjoy!

TIP Try this project in various color combinations to create different looks. Black and orange are great for Halloween. Try brown and red for an updated, rustic holiday look. White and gray would be beautiful for a winter dinner party. Get creative and enjoy—it's just paint!

TEMPLATES

Size as desired for your project.

Use transfer paper to transfer the design to your pot. Remember, the beauty of hand lettering is that you don't have to be exact. Make these designs your own!

provence

oh la la!

knives

forks

Spoons

Sage

mint

thyme